The Pooh Cook Book

Inspired by WINNIE-THE-POOH and
THE HOUSE AT POOH CORNER by A. A. MILNE

Recipes by KATIE STEWART
Illustrated by ERNEST SHEPARD

A Magnet Book

Also in Magnet Books:
WINNIE-THE-POOH
THE HOUSE AT POOH CORNER
WHEN WE WERE VERY YOUNG
NOW WE ARE SIX

Full-colour picture paperbacks:
THE POOH STORY BOOK
THE CHRISTOPHER ROBIN VERSE BOOK
PIGLET PAPERBACKS

First published in Great Britain 1971
by Methuen Children's Books Ltd
Reprinted seven times
Reprinted 1981
Magnet edition first published 1979
by Methuen Children's Books Ltd
11 New Fetter Lane, London EC4P 4EE
Reprinted three times
Reprinted 1985 (twice)
Individual copyright for text and illustrations:
Winnie-the-Pooh copyright 1926
The House at Pooh Corner copyright 1928
Recipes copyright © 1971 Katie Stewart
All rights reserved
Printed in Great Britain by
Hazell Watson & Viney Limited,
Member of the BPCC Group,
Aylesbury, Bucks

ISBN 0 416 88360 5

Contents

*The recipes which are marked * are the easiest to make*

PROVISIONS FOR PICNICS AND EXPOTITIONS

LUNCHES AND SUPPERS

DESSERT AND PARTY RECIPES

CHRISTMAS SPECIALITIES

HOT AND COLD DRINKS

Introduction by Katie Stewart

This is a cookery book with recipes specially chosen for you to enjoy, even if you've never cooked before. The recipes are set out under different headings, some for snacks, others for lunch or supper, and special ones for parties and to make at Christmas time. You can make tasty dishes for your friends, cakes for tea – even Winnie-the-Pooh's own birthday cake with pink sugar icing – or just cook for yourself for the fun of it. Some of the recipes are very easy ones, others a little more difficult. Start with the easy ones, they're marked on the contents page, and don't forget to read the page of helpful hints before you start.

As you look through the book you will notice that every recipe has a quotation from Winnie-the-Pooh. Pooh enjoyed his food and never needed an excuse to have 'a little something'. I know that he would have especially enjoyed the honey recipes in this book and I think you will find lots of your favourite recipes too. If you've never read A. A. Milne's stories, why not start by reading a chapter every night. Then when you know the adventures well, you can guess which story the extract comes from.

Enjoy yourself when you cook, go slowly and carefully, remembering that cooking is something very personal and the more care and thought you put into it the better the results will be. And have fun!

Helpful Hints

Cooking, like most things, is easy when you do it properly. Here are some useful points to remember:

Always read a recipe through carefully before you start to see you understand it and have everything you need.

Wash your hands, put on an apron and wipe down the table top where you will be working before you handle food.

Get out all the equipment you need before you start cooking and weigh or measure the ingredients carefully.

Turn on the oven – it takes about 15 minutes to heat up to the right temperature.

Don't hurry your cooking – remember knives are sharp, the oven and the saucepans may be very hot and it's a shame to spoil your enjoyment by having an accident.

Try to tidy and wash up as you go along so you are not left with a nasty mess at the end!

When you serve the food, decorate it and make it look as attractive as possible. This is fun to do and even seems to make things taste better.

How to 'rub in'

Cut the fat in pieces and add to the flour in the recipe. Then pick up small handfuls of the fat and flour mixture and holding your hands above the bowl, rub the fat into the flour using your thumbs and fingertips. As you rub, allow the mixture to fall through your fingers back into the bowl. Keep on doing this until the fat is evenly distributed through the mixture and the mixture looks like fine crumbs.

How to use a cutter

You may want to use a pastry cutter to cut out scones, biscuits or pastry circles. In each case, spoon a little extra flour to one side of your working surface. Dip the cutter in the flour each time before cutting the dough or pastry. This helps prevent the mixture from sticking to the cutter. With a plain cutter, press down and twist sharply to one side to make sure the dough is cut through, then lift away. With a fluted, or shaped cutter, press down firmly, but do not twist otherwise the decorative edges will be spoilt.

How to line a cake tin

To line a round cake tin, trace around the outside of the tin on greaseproof paper using a pencil. Then cut out the circle of paper using a pair of scissors. Grease the tin, place the paper inside and then grease the paper. To line an oblong shaped or loaf tin is no more difficult. Cut a strip of paper, the width of the base of the tin and long enough to cover the base and the two opposite sides. Grease the tin, place in the paper and grease the paper. Correctly cut, the paper should go into the tin at one end, along the base and out at the other end with a slight overlap so that you can get hold of it. When the cake or loaf is baked, loosen the unlined sides with a knife, then with the help of the paper ends lift the cake or loaf out.

Smackerels, Elevenses, and Teas

'Nearly eleven o'clock,' said Pooh happily.
'You're just in time for a little smackerel of
something. . . .'

The House at Pooh Corner

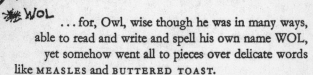

... for, Owl, wise though he was in many ways, able to read and write and spell his own name WOL, yet somehow went all to pieces over delicate words like MEASLES and BUTTERED TOAST.

Winnie-the-Pooh

Cinnamon Toast

Makes 6 toast slices
6 slices of white bread
butter for spreading

For the cinnamon sugar:
1 level tablespoon
   ground cinnamon
3 level tablespoons
   castor sugar

Find a small bowl and a tablespoon for mixing the cinnamon sugar, and a knife for cutting the cinnamon toast. Turn on the grill.

Toast the bread slices on both sides. While they are still hot, spread the slices with butter. Measure the cinnamon and sugar into a small bowl and mix together.

Sprinkle the cinnamon sugar generously over the buttered toast. Put the toast back under the hot grill, just for a few moments to melt the sugar.

Cut into fingers and serve.

Note: It's a good idea to make up the cinnamon sugar in advance. Keep it handy in a sugar sifter ready for use.

'I've been finding things in the Forest,' said Tigger importantly.
'I've found a pooh and a piglet and an eeyore, but I can't find
any breakfast.'
The House at Pooh Corner

Banana and Honey Spread

Enough for 4 large slices of bread
1 oz butter
1 tablespoon honey
2 ripe bananas
4 slices of brown or white bread from a large sliced loaf

Make sure the butter is not hard from the refrigerator. If it is, let
it stand until soft enough to beat with a spoon. Find a small
mixing bowl, a wooden spoon, a plate, a fork for mashing the
bananas and a knife for spreading.

Measure the butter and honey into a mixing bowl. Using a
wooden spoon, beat together until light and creamy.

Peel the bananas and mash on a plate using a fork. Add the
banana to the butter and honey and mix well.

Spread the mixture generously on the slices of bread. Cut each
slice into quarters and serve.

Pooh's Raisin Bread for Eating with Honey

Makes 1 large loaf
12 oz (or 12 rounded tablespoons) self raising flour
½ level teaspoon salt
3 oz (or 3 rounded tablespoons) castor sugar
1½ oz (about 24) walnut halves
3 tablespoons seedless raisins
2 eggs
just under ½ pint milk
2 oz butter
For the glaze: 1 tablespoon castor sugar
1 tablespoon milk

Find a large bowl, a sieve and a wooden spoon for mixing the bread, a small bowl for mixing the eggs, and a small saucepan for melting the butter and making the glaze. You will also need a pair of scissors and a pastry brush. Find a loaf tin about 9″ × 5″ × 2″

'When you wake up in the morning, Pooh,' said Piglet, 'what's
the first thing you say to yourself?'
'What's for breakfast?' said Pooh.

Winnie-the-Pooh

and grease it lightly. Turn on oven heat to moderate (350 °F or
Gas No 4) and find a pair of oven gloves.

Sift the flour and salt into a large bowl and add the sugar. Cut
up the walnuts coarsely using the scissors and add to the flour
together with the raisins. Stir well and hollow out the centre of
the mixture. Melt the butter in a saucepan over low heat. Lightly
mix the eggs.

Pour the eggs into the centre of the flour mixture and add the
milk. Using a wooden spoon mix to a soft dough. Stir in the
melted butter and mix thoroughly.

Pour into the greased loaf tin and spread evenly. Place in the
centre of the preheated oven and bake for 1 hour.

To give your loaf a shiny, professional looking finish, prepare
a glaze to brush over the top. About 5 minutes before the loaf is
cooked, measure 1 tablespoon castor sugar and 1 tablespoon milk
into a saucepan. Heat gently until the sugar dissolves, then bring
up to the boil. Simmer for a moment and draw off the heat.

Remove the baked loaf from the oven, using oven gloves, and
turn out of the tin. Using a pastry brush, brush the loaf all over
with the hot glaze to make it shiny.

Leave until cold, then serve sliced with butter and honey.

It's very, very funny,
'Cos I know I had some honey;
'Cos it has a label on
    Saying HUNNY.
               Winnie-the-Pooh

Honey and Raisin Scones

Makes 9–12 scones
8 oz (or 8 rounded tablespoons) self raising flour
½ level teaspoon salt
1 oz butter or margarine
1 level tablespoon castor sugar
2 tablespoons seedless raisins
1 tablespoon honey
1 egg
4 tablespoons milk (see recipe)

Find a mixing bowl, a sieve, and a fork for mixing the scones, a measuring jug, a 2″ round cutter or a knife for cutting the scones, and a baking tray. Turn on oven heat to hot (400 °F or Gas No 6) and find a pair of oven gloves.

Sift the flour and salt into a mixing bowl. Add the butter and rub into the mixture. Add the sugar and raisins, mix well and make a hollow in the centre.

Spoon the honey into a measuring jug, add the egg and suffi-
cient milk to make the liquid up to $\frac{1}{4}$ pint. Mix well with a fork.

Pour the honey, egg and milk into the centre of the flour and,
using a fork, mix to a rough dough in the basin. Turn out on to a
floured working surface and knead lightly to a smooth dough.

Pat or lightly roll the dough out to about $\frac{1}{2}''$ in thickness –
never make scone dough too thin. Use a floured round cutter to
stamp out 9–12 scones (don't waste the trimmings). Or cut the
dough neatly into squares with a knife.

Lightly flour the baking tray. Arrange the scones neatly on the
tray and dust the scones with flour. Place on a high shelf in the
preheated oven and bake for 12 minutes.

Serve warm with butter.

'Many a bear going out on a warm day like this would never have thought of bringing a little something with him.'

Winnie-the-Pooh

Gingernuts

Makes 16

4 oz (or 4 rounded tablespoons) plain flour
¼ level teaspoon salt
1 level teaspoon baking powder
1 level teaspoon bicarbonate of soda
1 level teaspoon ground ginger
1 level teaspoon ground mixed spice
2 oz butter or margarine
2 oz (or 2 rounded tablespoons) castor sugar
1 heaped tablespoon golden syrup

Find a mixing bowl, a sieve, a wooden spoon and a small saucepan. You will also need a saucer to hold the sugar for coating the gingernuts and a tumbler to squash them flat. Find a baking tray and grease it lightly, and a wire cooling tray. Turn on the oven heat to moderate (350 °F or Gas No 4) and find a pair of oven gloves.

Sift together the flour, salt, baking powder, bicarbonate of soda, ginger and mixed spice into a mixing basin. Add the butter or margarine and rub into the mixture. Stir in the sugar.

Measure the syrup into a saucepan and warm over low heat until it is runny but not too hot. Pour it all at once into the flour mixture, and mix with a wooden spoon to make a soft dough.

Turn the dough out on to a clean working surface and shape into a long sausage. Cut the sausage in half and then each piece into half again. Now cut each portion of dough into four and you should have 16 equal sized pieces of dough.

Using the palms of your hands, roll each piece of dough into a ball. Place about 2 tablespoons castor sugar in a saucer and roll each ball of dough in the sugar to coat it. Then place well apart on the greased baking tray. Put only about 6 on the baking tray at once – these gingernuts spread flat while baking and are best cooked in batches. Flatten each gingernut with the base of a tumbler dipped in the castor sugar.

Place the gingernuts in the centre of the preheated oven and bake for 15 minutes. Remove from the oven using oven gloves and allow to cool on the tray for a few moments. Then using a palette knife lift them off the tray on to a wire cooling tray.

When cold and crisp, store in an airtight tin.

Chocolate Krinkles

Makes 12
4 oz plain chocolate
small nut of vegetable fat
3 teacupfuls cornflakes
2 tablespoons sultanas

Find a large saucepan and a mixing bowl that will fit snugly over
the top for melting the chocolate and mixing, a spoon, and 12
paper cases. Set the paper cases on a flat plate or preferably in bun
tins so that they don't move around when you spoon in the
mixture. Half fill the saucepan with hot water and set the basin
over the top.

Break the chocolate into the basin and add the vegetable fat.
(This helps to thin the chocolate down so it will coat the cornflakes more evenly.) Leave the basin of chocolate over the heat,
stirring occasionally until the chocolate has melted and the
mixture is smooth.

Sing Ho! for a Bear
Sing Ho! for Pooh
And I'll have a little
something in an
hour or two!
Winnie-the-Pooh

Remove the basin from the heat and add the cornflakes and sultanas to the melted chocolate. Using a metal spoon, mix the ingredients gently but thoroughly so that the cornflakes are all coated with chocolate.

Spoon heaped tablespoons of the mixture into the 12 paper cases. Set aside in a cool place, the refrigerator is ideal, until quite firm.

'Let's go and see everybody,' said Pooh. 'Because
when you have been walking in the wind for miles,
and you suddenly go into somebody's house, and he
says, "Hallo, Pooh you're just in time for a little
smackerel of something," and you are, then it's what
I call a Friendly Day.'

The House at Pooh Corner

Chocolate Peanut Squares

Makes 12

4 oz plain chocolate
2 rounded tablespoons crunchy style peanut butter
3 teacupfuls rice crispies

Find a large saucepan and a mixing bowl that will fit snugly over
the top for melting the chocolate and mixing, a wooden
spoon and a 7″ shallow square tin. Lightly grease the tin. Half
fill the saucepan with hot water, and set the basin over the
top.

Break the chocolate into the basin and add the peanut butter.
Leave the basin over the heat until the chocolate has melted, then
stir to blend the chocolate and peanut butter.

Remove the basin from the heat and add the rice crispies. Using
a wooden spoon, gently stir the crispies until they are completely
coated with the chocolate mixture.

Spoon the mixture into the greased tin, spread evenly and press down firmly. Leave in a cool place, a refrigerator is best, until quite firm.

Remove from the tin and cut into squares.

Honey Spice Cake

Makes 24 squares

7 oz (or 7 rounded tablespoons) self raising flour
1 level teaspoon mixed spice
½ level teaspoon ground ginger
½ level teaspoon ground cinnamon
5 oz butter or margarine
4 oz (or 4 rounded tablespoons) soft brown sugar
6 oz (or 3 rounded tablespoons) honey
2 eggs
1 tablespoon water

Find a sieve, a square of foil or greaseproof paper, a saucepan and a wooden spoon. Take an oblong cake tin of about 11″ × 7″ × 1″ or a small roasting tin, grease the tin and line with a strip of greaseproof paper. Turn the oven heat on to moderate (350 °F or Gas No 4) and find a pair of oven gloves.

Sift together the flour, mixed spice, ginger and cinnamon on to a square of greaseproof paper or foil and set aside.

... his nose told him it was indeed honey, and his tongue
came out and began to polish up his mouth, ready for it.

Winnie-the-Pooh

Measure the butter or margarine, and the sugar, honey and
water into a saucepan. Place the pan over a low heat and stir with
a wooden spoon until the fat has melted. Do not allow to boil.
Draw the pan off the heat and allow to cool for about ten minutes.

Using a wooden spoon, beat the eggs into the honey mixture
one at a time. Tip in the flour mixture all at once. Stir until it has
blended and then beat thoroughly.

Pour into the prepared cake tin and spread evenly. Place in the
centre of the preheated oven and bake for 30–35 minutes or until
the cake is well risen.

Remove the cake from the oven using oven gloves. Loosen the
sides of the cake with a knife and turn out. Allow to cool and then
cut in squares.

'Well,' said Pooh, 'at eleven o'clock – at eleven o'clock – well, at eleven o'clock, you see I generally get home about then. Because I have One or Two Things to Do.'
The House at Pooh Corner

Biscuit Cake

Cuts into 12 portions
½ lb rich tea biscuits
4 oz butter or margarine
1½ oz (or 3 rounded tablespoons) cocoa powder
2 oz (or 2 rounded tablespoons) castor sugar
1 heaped tablespoon golden syrup
4 oz plain chocolate

Find a knife, a board for cutting, a large saucepan and a wooden spoon for mixing the cake. Choose an 8″ round sponge cake tin and butter it well. Line across the base with a folded strip of foil about 2″ wide – this makes the chilled cake easier to remove afterwards. You will also need a smaller saucepan and a bowl that will fit snugly over the top of it for melting the chocolate. Half fill the saucepan with hot water and set the bowl over the top.

Cut the biscuits up coarsely with a knife. Measure the butter or margarine, the cocoa powder, sugar and syrup into a large saucepan. Place the saucepan over a low heat, and using a wooden

spoon, stir occasionally until the ingredients have melted and blended. Draw the pan off the heat.

Tip in all the biscuits at once. Using a fork, stir until the ingredients are blended and the biscuits are coated with the chocolate mixture.

Spoon the mixture into the prepared cake tin. Spread level and press the mixture firmly into the tin.

Break the chocolate into the bowl which you have set over the saucepan of hot water. Leave over the hot water until the chocolate has melted, stir occasionally until smooth. Remove the bowl from the heat.

Spoon the melted chocolate on top of the biscuit cake and using a knife spread evenly over the whole surface. Place the cake in the refrigerator and chill until set quite firm.

Loosen the edges of the cake using a knife and lift the cake out of the tin using the foil to help. Cut into wedges and serve.

Winnie-the-Pooh came over all funny, and had to hurry home
for a little snack of something to sustain him.

Winnie-the-Pooh

Drop Scones

Makes 24

8 oz (or 8 rounded tablespoons) self raising flour
½ level teaspoon salt
½ oz butter
1 oz (or 1 rounded tablespoon) castor sugar
1 egg
1 dessertspoon golden syrup
⅓ pint (or 1 teacupful) milk

Find a medium-sized mixing bowl, a sieve, a wooden spoon for
mixing and a small bowl for the egg. You will also need a large
heavy-based frying pan, a dessertspoon and a palette knife for
cooking the scones and a clean tea-cloth to keep them warm.

Sift the flour and salt into a mixing basin. Add the butter and
rub into the mixture. Add the sugar, stir well and hollow out the
centre of the ingredients.

Crack the egg into a small bowl, add the syrup and mix together with a fork. Pour the egg mixture into the centre of the

flour and add the milk. Using a wooden spoon, stir the mixture from the centre gradually drawing in the flour from around the sides of the bowl. Mix to a thick batter. Add a further tablespoon of milk if the mixture is too thick – it should feel like heavy cream.

Lightly grease the frying pan with a buttered paper and set over moderate heat. When the pan is hot, drop the mixture by dessert-spoonfuls on to the surface. Cook gently and when bubbles start to burst on the surface and the underside is brown, turn over and cook on the second side for a few moments.

Cook the scones in batches and as they are ready, lift them from the pan and place in a folded cloth to keep them warm. Grease the pan each time with the buttered paper before cooking the next batch of scones. As the pan gets hot it is best to hold the paper with an oven glove.

Serve the drop scones warm with butter and jam or, of course, honey.

Slice and Bake Cookies

Makes about 4 dozen cookies
6 oz (or 6 rounded tablespoons) plain flour
¼ level teaspoon bicarbonate of soda
½ level teaspoon salt
4 oz butter or margarine
4 oz (or 4 rounded tablespoons) castor sugar
1 egg
few drops vanilla essence
2 oz (or 2 rounded tablespoons) finely chopped walnuts

Find a bowl, a sieve, a wooden spoon for mixing, a knife for cutting, and foil to wrap the dough. You will also need a baking tray and a pair of oven gloves.

Sift together the flour, bicarbonate of soda and salt on to a plate and set aside. Measure the butter or margarine and sugar into a mixing bowl and using a wooden spoon, beat the mixture until it is smooth and pale in colour.

Crack the egg into a small bowl, add the vanilla essence and

Some hours later, just as the night was beginning to steal away, Pooh woke up suddenly with a sinking feeling. He had had that sinking feeling before, and he knew what it meant. *He was hungry.*

Winnie-the-Pooh

beat lightly with a fork. Gradually beat the egg into the fat and sugar, a little at a time. Stir in the sifted dry ingredients and the chopped nuts. Mix thoroughly.

Turn the dough out on to a lightly floured working surface. Divide the dough in half and, using lightly floured hands, shape each piece into a fat roll about 6″ long. Place each piece of dough in the centre of a square of kitchen foil. Fold the foil tightly over the dough and twist the ends like a cracker.

Place the dough in the refrigerator to chill. These cookies are the sort that you slice off and bake when you feel like 'a little something'.

When ready to use, carefully unwrap one piece of the dough. Then, using a sharp knife, slice off as many cookies as required. Cut the dough in about ¼″ thick slices. Rewrap the remaining dough and return to the refrigerator.

Place the cookies on a lightly greased baking tray and place in the centre of a moderate oven (350 °F or Gas No 4) and bake for 15 minutes.

'And the only reason for making honey is so
as I can eat it.'

Winnie-the-Pooh

Gingerbread Men

Makes 12

8 oz (or 8 rounded tablespoons) plain flour
1 level teaspoon baking powder
2 level teaspoons ground ginger
1 level teaspoon ground cinnamon
2 oz butter or margarine
2 oz (or 2 rounded tablespoons) soft brown sugar
2 heaped tablespoons golden syrup
few currants for decoration

Find a medium-sized mixing bowl, a sieve, a saucepan, a wooden
spoon, a pastry board and a knife for cutting. You will also need
two baking trays, a palette knife and a wire cooling tray. Grease
the baking trays, turn on the oven to moderate heat (350 °F or
Gas No 4) and find a pair of oven gloves.

Sift together the flour, baking powder, ginger and cinnamon
into a medium-sized mixing bowl.

Measure the butter or margarine, brown sugar and golden
syrup into a saucepan. Place over a low heat and stir occasionally

until the ingredients have melted and the mixture is runny but not too hot. Draw the pan off the heat.

Pour the melted mixture into the flour all at once. Using a wooden spoon, mix to a dough in the basin, then turn out on to a floured working surface and knead lightly until smooth. The dough should be fairly soft and easy to mould. If it seems very soft, allow it to stand for a few moments to firm up.

Cut the dough into half and set one half aside. Cut the remaining piece of dough in half again, to make two smaller pieces. Using floured hands, shape the pieces for the gingerbread men as follows:

Divide one of the smaller pieces of dough equally into 12 and roll each bit into a ball to make the heads.

Divide the second small piece of dough equally into 12, then roll into a sausage and nip the sausage in half. From each piece make two small arms and two small legs for each man.

Take the large piece of dough which you had set aside, and divide equally into 12 pieces. Shape each piece into a long fat body.

Put the men together on the baking trays. If you have only one baking tray, shape some on the board ready for baking. Press a body, a head and the right number of arms and legs on each man. Press some currants down the tummy for buttons and, if you like, give each man two currant eyes.

Place the tray in the centre of the oven and bake for 10–12 minutes or until golden brown. Remove the tray from the oven using oven gloves and loosen each man carefully with a palate knife. Place on a wire cooling tray and bake the remaining gingerbread men.

Provisions for Picnics and Expotitions

'Oh! Piglet,' said Pooh excitedly 'we're going on a Expotition, all of us, with things to eat To discover something.'

Winnie-the-Pooh

Now it happened that Kanga
had felt rather motherly that morning,
and Wanting to Count Things – like Roo's vests, and how many pieces
of soap there were left, and the two clean spots in Tigger's feeder; so
she had sent them out with a packet of watercress sandwiches for Roo...

The House at Pooh Corner

Watercress Sandwiches

Makes 4 rounds of sandwiches
8 slices of white bread, taken from a large sliced loaf
butter for spreading
little Marmite
1 bunch watercress

Find a cutting board and a small knife for spreading.

Lay the slices of bread out neatly on a board. Lightly butter
each one. Spread four of the slices with just a little Marmite.
Thoroughly wash the watercress and strip the leaves off the
stems. Arrange the watercress leaves over the four slices of bread.
Cover with the remaining four slices and press gently. Trim away
the crusts and cut the sandwiches across into squares.

It was a warm day,
and he had a long way to go.
He hadn't gone more than half-way when a sort of funny feeling began to creep all over him. It began at the tip of his nose and trickled all through him and out at the soles of his feet. It was just as if somebody inside him were saying, 'Now then, Pooh, time for a little something.'

Winnie-the-Pooh

Crispie Squares

Makes 10–12 squares

¼ lb white marshmallows   ¼ lb butter or margarine
¼ lb cream caramels   1 small (6oz.) packet rice crispies

Find a large saucepan, a wooden spoon and a shallow tin – a small roasting tin is a good choice.

Put the marshmallows, butter or margarine and cream caramels into a saucepan. Place over a low heat and stir gently until the ingredients have melted and the mixture is blended. Draw the pan off the heat.

Add the rice crispies all at once and stir gently until the crispies are coated in the toffee mixture. Pour into a shallow tin and press the mixture down evenly.

Leave in a cool place until the mixture has set firm, then cut in squares.

Egg Sandwiches

Makes 4 rounds of sandwiches
8 slices of brown or white bread taken from a large sliced loaf
butter for spreading
For the filling:
3 large eggs
½ oz butter
salt and pepper
1 tablespoon creamy milk

Find a cutting board and a bowl, a table knife and a spoon.

Lay the slices of bread out neatly on the board. Lightly butter each one and set aside while preparing the filling.

Place the eggs in a saucepan and cover with cold water. Bring up to the boil and simmer for 8 minutes to hard boil them. Drain the eggs and cover with cold water. As soon as the eggs are cool enough to handle, peel away the shells.

Place the warm eggs in a mixing bowl with the butter. Using a table knife, chop the eggs in the bowl. The butter will melt with

Roo was silent for a little while, and then he said,
'Shall we eat our sandwiches, Tigger?' And Tigger
said, 'Yes, where are they?'

The House at Pooh Corner

the heat of the eggs. Season with salt and pepper and mix in the milk. This makes a nice filling that sets a little on cooling and will not fall out of the sandwiches.

Dividing the egg mixture equally, spoon on to 4 of the buttered bread slices. Spread evenly and place a second slice, buttered side down, on top. Press together. Trim away the crusts, and cut each sandwich diagonally in half.

'Well,' said Pooh, 'I could stay a little longer if it – if you—'
and he tried very hard to look in the direction of the larder.
Winnie-the-Pooh

Layer Sandwiches

Makes 20 small sandwiches
4 slices white bread, taken from a large sliced loaf
4 slices brown bread, taken from a large sliced loaf
butter for spreading
For the fillings:
1 tin of sardines
squeeze of lemon juice
1 small packet cream cheese
salt and pepper
2 hard boiled eggs (made by bringing the eggs to the boil in a
saucepan of water and leaving to simmer for 8 minutes.)
1 tablespoon salad cream

Find a board, a table knife, a fork, three small bowls for mixing
the fillings, and a spoon.

Lay the slices of bread out neatly on the board. Lightly butter
each one and set aside. Prepare each of the fillings in separate
small bowls as follows:

Drain the sardines from the tin. Remove the tails and then mash

the sardines with a fork adding a little lemon juice. Check the taste.

Mix the cream cheese in a small bowl until soft and season lightly with salt and pepper.

Mash the hard boiled eggs thoroughly with a fork and mix in the salad cream.

Take two slices of the white bread and spread both with the sardine filling. Top with two slices of brown bread and spread these with the cream cheese filling. Top with two slices of white bread and spread these with the egg filling. Finally top with the remaining two slices of brown bread buttered sides inwards. Press gently together.

At this stage it is best to let the two stacks of sandwiches stand for about 30 minutes before cutting. In any case, they keep nice and moist this way and should only be cut when ready for serving.

Using a sharp knife, cut downwards round each stack, removing all the crusts. Cut each stack in half across the centre to make two sandwich strips. Now slice across and down each strip to get 5 dainty small sandwiches, with a stripy filling from each one.
Note: These sandwiches are almost too pretty for a picnic, make them for party or for tea when friends next visit you.

Picnic Loaf

Serves 4
1 small Vienna loaf
butter for spreading
3–4 washed lettuce leaves
2 tomatoes
1 (7½ oz) tin tuna fish
1–2 tablespoons salad cream
few snipped chives

Find a bread knife for cutting and a table knife for spreading. You
will also need a tin opener, a small bowl and a fork.

Using a bread knife, cut the Vienna loaf in half lengthwise. Be
careful with the knife. Butter the inside of both halves.

Arrange the washed lettuce leaves along the bottom slice. Wash
and slice the tomatoes and arrange these on top.

Open the tin of tuna fish and drain away the oil. Tip the flesh
into a mixing bowl and flake the fish with a fork. Add the salad
cream and chives and stir lightly to mix.

'. . . And we must all bring Provisions.'
'Bring what?'
'Things to eat.'
'Oh!' said Pooh happily. 'I thought you said
Provisions. I'll go and tell them.'
                                    Winnie-the-Pooh

Pile the tuna filling along the length of the loaf on top of the tomato. Spread fairly evenly. Top with the remaining slice of bread and press down.

Before serving, cut into four chunky slices. For a picnic, wrap loosely in foil for carrying, and cut when ready to eat.

Flapjack

Makes 8 pieces

2 oz butter or margarine
1 rounded tablespoon golden syrup
2 oz (or 2 rounded tablespoons) soft brown sugar
4 oz (or 8 heaped tablespoons) rolled oats
pinch of salt

Find a saucepan, a wooden spoon and a 7″ sponge cake tin. Grease the sponge cake tin and turn on the oven heat to moderate (350 °F or Gas No 4). Find a pair of oven gloves.

Measure the butter, or margarine, syrup and sugar into a saucepan. Place over a low heat and stir occasionally with a wooden spoon until the butter has melted and the mixture is blended. Draw the pan off the heat.

Add the oats and salt and mix well. Spoon the mixture into the prepared tin and press evenly. Place in the centre of the pre-heated moderate oven and bake for 20 minutes.

'It's like this,' he said. 'When you are after honey with
a ballon, the great thing is not to let the bees know
you're coming.'

Winnie-the-Pooh

When baked, remove from the oven and, holding the tin in
an oven glove, mark the flapjack into 8 neat divisions with a
knife.

Allow to cool, then remove from the tin and break into pieces.
If not eaten at once, store any left over in an airtight tin.

. . . they stayed there until very nearly tea-time, and then they had a Very Nearly tea, which is one you forget about afterwards.

House at Pooh Corner

Home-made Bread Rolls

Makes 12 rolls

1 lb plain flour
2 level teaspoons salt
¼ oz lard or vegetable fat
½ pint warm water (see recipe)
1 level teaspoon sugar
¼ oz (or 2 level teaspoons) dried yeast
beaten egg and milk for glazing
poppy seeds for decoration (optional)

Find a large mixing bowl, a sieve, a wooden spoon, a measuring jug, a knife, two baking trays and a pastry brush. At a later stage you will need to turn on the oven heat to hot (425 °F or Gas No 7) and you should grease the baking trays. You will also need a pair of oven gloves.

Sift the flour and salt into a large mixing bowl. Add the fat and rub into the mixture. Hollow out the centre of the ingredients.

Measure the water carefully. The water should be hand hot, in other words you should be able to hold a finger in it quite comfortably – get the right temperature by mixing hot water from the kettle and cold water from the tap. Stir in the sugar and then sprinkle the yeast over the top. Set aside in a warm place for about 10 minutes or until the yeast mixture froths up like beer.

Pour the yeast all at once into the centre of the flour mixture. Using your hands mix the ingredients to a rough dough in the basin. Turn out on to a clean working surface and knead and flatten the dough for about 10 minutes. Work until the dough is nice and elastic and no longer sticky.

Divide the dough in half and then divide each half into 6 equal pieces so that you have 12 pieces in all. Roll up each piece into a round and allow to rest for 10 minutes.

Roll out each piece of dough to an even rope, the length depending on the shape of roll you wish to make.

Single knot: Roll an 8″ length rope of dough and tie loosely in a single knot.

Twin knot: Roll out a 12″ rope of dough. Bring each end up and over to make two loops, then tuck the ends through the loops.

Coils: Roll out a 12″ rope of dough. Coil up neatly from one end. Secure the last piece by pinching two strands together on the underside.

Esses: Roll out a 12″ rope of dough. Coil up neatly from each end. One coil being above the rope of dough and the other being below.

As you prepare each roll place it neatly on the baking tray. Brush each one with the mixture of beaten egg and milk, then set in a warm place covered with a cloth until risen and puffy.

When ready to bake, brush tops again with a little more egg and milk. Sprinkle some poppy seeds over the tops. Place in the centre of a very hot oven and bake for 20–25 minutes.

When cold, spread rolls with butter, and fill with cheese, lettuce, tomato or any other filling you like.

Isn't it funny
How a bear likes honey
Buzz! Buzz! Buzz!
I wonder why he does
Winnie-the-Pooh

Honey Cookies

Makes about 30
8 oz (or 8 rounded tablespoons) self raising flour
pinch of salt
4 oz butter or margarine
4 oz (or 4 rounded tablespoons) soft brown sugar
1 egg
1 rounded tablespoon honey
few drops vanilla essence
flaked almonds to decorate

Find a plate, a medium-sized and a small mixing bowl, and a wooden spoon for mixing. Find a baking tray and grease it, and a teaspoon to shape the cookies. Turn on the oven heat to moderate (350 °F or Gas No 4). You will also need a wire cooling tray and a pair of oven gloves.

Sift the flour and salt on to a plate and set aside. Measure the butter and sugar into a medium-sized mixing basin and using a wooden spoon, beat it well until soft. Crack the egg into a small basin, add the vanilla essence and mix lightly.

Gradually beat the egg into the butter and sugar, a little at a time. Beat in the honey. Add half the sifted flour and mix to a soft dough. Add the remaining flour and mix to a firm dough.

Spoon out rounded teaspoons of the mixture and roll into balls. Place these, about 6–8 at a time on a greased baking tray. Flatten each cookie slightly with your fingers and top each one with a piece of flaked almond.

Place the cookies in the centre of the preheated oven and bake for 12 minutes. When baked remove from the heat using oven gloves. Then, with a palette knife, lift each cookie off the tray on to a cooling rack. Now bake the next batch of cookies and continue until all the dough is used up.

'I think,' said Christopher Robin, 'that we ought
to eat all our Provisions now, so that we shan't have
so much to carry.'
'Eat all our what?' said Pooh.
'All that we've brought,' said Piglet, getting to work.

Winnie-the-Pooh

Chocolate Rock Cakes

Makes 12
8 oz (or 8 rounded tablespoons) self raising flour
pinch of salt
3 oz butter or margarine
4 oz plain chocolate
3 oz (or 3 rounded tablespoons) castor sugar
1 egg
2 tablespoons milk
few drops vanilla essence

Find two forks, a knife, a board for cutting, a medium-sized and
a small bowl for mixing. Find a baking tray and grease it, turn on
the oven heat to moderate (350 °F or Gas No 4) and find a pair of
oven gloves.

Sift the flour and salt into a large mixing basin. Add the butter
or margarine, cut in pieces and rub into the mixture. Using a
knife cut the chocolate fairly coarsely and add to the flour along
with the sugar. Mix well and make a hollow in the centre.

Crack the egg into a small bowl, add the milk and the vanilla essence and mix lightly. Add all at once to the centre of the flour mixture, and using a fork mix to a rough dough. The mixture will be fairly stiff.

Using two forks, pile the mixture in rough heaps on the greased baking tray, not too close together. You should get about 12 on one baking tray, but if the tray is small then bake in batches of 6.

Place in the centre of the preheated hot oven and bake for 10–15 minutes or until lightly browned. Remove from the heat using oven gloves, then loosen the rock cakes with a palette knife and lift on to a wire cooling tray. Leave until cold.

Lunches and Suppers

'Anyhow,' he said, 'it is nearly Luncheon Time.'
So he went home for it.

Winnie-the-Pooh

... he was so tired when he got home that, in the very middle of his supper, after he had been eating for little more than half-an-hour, he fell fast asleep . . . .

Winnie-the-Pooh

Toasted Bacon Sandwiches

Serves 4
8 slices of bread from a large sliced loaf
butter for spreading
tomato ketchup
2 oz (or 2 heaped tablespoons) grated cheese
6 bacon rashers

Find a board for cutting, a pair of scissors and a knife.

Toast the bread on both sides and while hot spread with butter. Spread 4 of the slices with a little tomato ketchup and sprinkle with the cheese.

Using a pair of scissors, trim the rinds from the bacon rashers and then cut each rasher in half. Arrange the pieces of bacon neatly over the toast slices to cover the cheese.

Replace the slices under the hot grill, about 3″ from the heat. Grill until the cheese has melted and the bacon cooked. Remove from the heat and top with the other four slices of toast, buttered side inwards. Press together to make a sandwich and serve.

So he took his largest pot of honey and escaped with
it to a broad branch of his tree, well above the water,
and then he climbed down again and escaped with another
pot . . . .

Winnie-the-Pooh

French Toast with Honey

Serves 4

5 slices of white bread taken from a large sliced loaf
2 eggs
2 tablespoons of milk
2 oz butter for frying

Find a fork, a shallow dish, a frying pan, and a plate for serving.

Trim away the crusts from the bread slices and cut each slice
across, into 3 fingers. Crack the eggs into a shallow dish, add the
milk and beat lightly with a fork.

Melt half the butter in a frying pan. Dip the bread fingers, one at
a time, both sides in the egg mixture. Drain for a moment and then
add to the hot butter. Add only as many as the pan will hold easily.

Fry the bread fingers, turning them once or twice until golden
brown on both sides. Lift from the pan, arrange on a hot plate,
and keep warm. Fry all the bread slices in the same way adding
the remaining butter to the pan as you need it.

Serve hot with honey.

... they left the basket under the trees and went back to dinner.

The House at Pooh Corner

Baked Stuffed Potatoes

Serves 4

4 large even sized potatoes
2 oz butter
salt and pepper
4 bacon rashers

Find a mixing bowl, a fork, a spoon and a pair of scissors. Get out a small saucepan and a baking tray. Turn on the oven heat to hot (400 °F or Gas No 6). Don't forget that potatoes can be baked along with something else. Make sure you have a pair of oven gloves.

Scrub the potatoes and then dry them. Prick all over with a fork and then place the potatoes on a baking tray. Place in the centre of the oven and bake for $1-1\frac{1}{2}$ hours depending on the size. When ready they should feel soft when pressed.

Meanwhile, using a pair of scissors, trim the rinds from the bacon rashers and then cut the rashers in pieces. Place in a saucepan and fry over a low heat until the fat runs and the bacon bits are cooked. Remove from the heat.

Take the baked potatoes out of the oven. Hold each potato with your oven glove and cut in half. Using a spoon, scoop out the soft middle into a mixing basin. Set the potato shells carefully aside in pairs.

Add half the butter, a seasoning of salt and pepper and the bacon to the hot potato. Mix together using a fork. Spoon the mixture back into the potato shells, fork it neatly and then dot with bits of the remaining butter.

Rearrange the potatoes on the baking tin and reheat in the oven, or place them under a hot grill to brown. Serve hot.

Toad in the Hole

Serves 4

1 lb beef or pork sausages
½ oz lard, dripping or vegetable fat
For the batter:
4 oz (or 4 rounded tablespoons) plain flour
¼ level teaspoon salt
1 egg
½ pint milk

Find a roasting tin, a sieve, a bowl for mixing and a wooden spoon. Turn on oven heat to hot (400 °F or Gas No 6) and find a pair of oven gloves.

Place the sausages in a medium-sized roasting tin and add the fat. Set aside while preparing the batter.

Sieve the flour and salt into a mixing bowl, and hollow out the centre. Crack the egg into the centre and add about one third of the milk. Using a wooden spoon, stir gently starting in the centre and gradually drawing in the flour from around the sides of the

'. . . suppose I get stuck in his front door again,
coming out, as I did once when his front door wasn't
big enough?'
'Because I know I'm not getting fatter, but his front
door may be getting thinner.'

The House at Pooh Corner

bowl. Add the remaining milk gradually, stirring all the time.
Beat well for 1 minute, to let air into the batter.

Place the sausages in the oven and leave for about 10 minutes
until the fat is very hot. Using oven gloves, remove the tin from
the oven and pour in the batter. Replace the tin in the oven, near
the top. Bake for 25–30 minutes, or until the batter is well risen
and crisp. Serve at once, cut in pieces.

'Could you ask your friend to do his exercises
somewhere else? I shall be having lunch directly,
and don't want it bounced on just before I begin . . .'
                        The House at Pooh Corner

Pizza

Serves 4
12 oz (or 12 rounded tablespoons) self raising flour
1 level teaspoon salt
2 oz butter or margarine
2 oz (or 2 heaped tablespoons) grated cheese
just under ½ pint milk to mix
For the topping:
1 oz butter or margarine
1 medium-sized onion
2 tablespoons tomato purée
pinch of mixed herbs
3 oz (or 3 heaped tablespoons) grated cheese
1 tin anchovy fillets

Find a bowl for mixing, a fork, a sieve and a grater for the cheese.
You will also need a small saucepan, a knife and a board for
cutting. Find a 3″ plain round cutter or a glass tumbler and a
baking tray. Turn on the oven heat to hot (425 °F or Gas No 7)
grease the baking tray and find a pair of oven gloves.

Sift the flour and salt into a bowl. Add the butter or margarine and rub into the mixture. Stir in the grated cheese and hollow out the centre of the ingredients.

Add the milk all at once and using a fork, mix to a rough dough in the basin. Turn the dough out on to a floured surface and knead lightly. Set aside to rest while you prepare the topping.

Melt the butter or margarine in a saucepan, add the onion and fry gently for about 5 minutes until the onion is soft. Stir in the tomato purée and the mixed herbs. Cook for a further few moments then draw off the heat.

Sprinkle a little flour on the working surface and roll out the dough to about $\frac{1}{2}''$ in thickness – take care not to roll it too thin. Using the 3" cutter, stamp out 8 rounds of dough – flour the cutter each time you use it. (You can, instead, use the tumbler as a guide and with a small knife, cut out the rounds of dough.)

Place the rounds of dough, which will now form the base for each pizza, on the baking tray. Spoon a little tomato topping on to each one and spread evenly. Sprinkle generously with the grated cheese.

Drain the anchovy fillets from the tin. The salty taste of anchovy fillets is rather nice, but if you prefer a milder flavour, put them to soak in a little milk before you start the recipe. Cut each anchovy in half lengthwise. Decorate each pizza with two strips of anchovy.

Place the tray of pizza on a high shelf in the hot oven and bake for 10–12 minutes, or until well risen and brown. Serve them hot and newly baked with salad.

Salad – Curls and Roses

Serves 4
1 small head of lettuce
few spring onions
3 tomatoes
2–3 new carrots
6 radishes
ice cubes from the refrigerator
For the dressing:
salt and pepper
1 level teaspoon castor sugar
2 tablespoons vinegar
4 tablespoons salad oil

Find a vegetable parer and a small sharp knife, a large bowl for iced water, a small bowl for the dressing, two spoons and a pretty bowl for serving the salad.

Remove any outer bruised leaves from the lettuce head, and separate the remaining leaves. Wash in cold water and then drain

He made up a little hum that very morning as he was
doing his Stoutness Exercises in front of the glass:
Tra-la-la, tra-la-la,
Tra-la-la, tra-la-la,
Rum-tum-tiddle-um-tum.

Winnie-the-Pooh

well. Trim the tops and base from the spring onions and wash
well. Wash the tomatoes and cut in quarters. You can put these in
a large polythene bag in the refrigerator to keep them fresh while
preparing the iced carrot sticks and radish roses.

Fill a bowl with cold water and add plenty of ice cubes. Using
a vegetable parer, thinly pare the carrots. Place the thin strips of
carrot in the iced water and after a little while they will curl up.
Trim the radishes and, using a small knife, cut from the tip to the
stalk end, not quite through, two or three times. Place in iced
water, after a little time these will open out into flowers.

Meanwhile prepare the dressing. In a small basin place a
sprinkle of salt and pepper. Add the sugar and stir in the vinegar –
the sugar helps to take away the harsh vinegar flavour. Add the
oil and mix well.

When ready to serve, place the lettuce, spring onions and
tomatoes in the salad bowl. Pour over the dressing and toss with
two spoons to mix well. Drain the carrot curls and the radish
roses from the iced water and use these to garnish the salad.

Potato Pancakes with Bacon

Serves 4

1 lb potatoes
1 onion
2 eggs
2 oz (or 2 rounded tablespoons) plain flour
1 level teaspoon salt
pinch of pepper
8 bacon rashers
2–3 tablespoons oil for frying

Find a potato peeler, a grater, a large mixing bowl, a wooden spoon for mixing and a tablespoon. Choose a large frying pan and find a pair of scissors for trimming the bacon rashers.

Peel the potatoes and the onion. Grate the potatoes and the onion, through the coarse side of a grater, into a large mixing basin. Take care not to grate your fingers! Add the eggs, the flour, salt and pepper and using a wooden spoon mix the ingredients thoroughly.

'Hallo, Owl,' said Pooh. 'I hope we're not too late for . . . I mean, how are you, Owl?'

The House at Pooh Corner

Using a pair of scissors, trim the rinds from the bacon rashers. Arrange the rashers neatly in the grill pan (remove the grid first). Place the fat part of each rasher overlapping the lean of the next and set aside ready for grilling.

Heat the oil in a frying pan and add the potato mixture in tablespoons at a time. Fry only 3–4 pancakes at a time and as you spoon the mixture in flatten them slightly.

Fry the pancakes over a moderate heat until brown on the underside – it should take about 5 minutes. Then turn over and brown the second side.

As the pancakes are cooked, lift from the pan and place on a hot serving plate. Keep the prepared ones warm, while cooking the remainder. You should get about 12 pancakes.

When they are almost all ready, turn on the grill. Place the bacon rashers under the grill, about 3″ from the heat, and grill for about 3–5 minutes.

Serve the hot pancakes, allowing about 3 per person, together with the grilled bacon rashers.

Sausage Turnovers

Serves 4

1 (7½ oz) packet frozen puff pastry, thawed
½ lb beef or pork chipolata sausages
milk for glazing
1 oz (or 1 heaped tablespoon) grated cheese

Make sure the pastry has thawed before trying to roll it out, it should stand for about 1 hour at room temperature. Find a pastry board, a rolling pin and a knife for the pastry. You will also need a pastry brush and a baking tray. Wet the baking tray by running it under the cold water tap – do not dry. Turn on the oven heat to hot (400 °F or Gas No 6) and find a pair of oven gloves.

Sprinkle a little flour on the pastry board and carefully roll out the pastry to approximately one 10″ square. Using a sharp knife trim the outside edges even and then cut the pastry across the middle to make 4 smaller 5″ squares. Cut each of these in half diagonally to make 2 triangles, giving 8 pieces of pastry in all.

Christopher Robin went
back to lunch with his friends Pooh and Piglet, and
on the way they told him of the Awful Mistake they had made.
The House at Pooh Corner

Separate the sausages. Using a pastry brush, brush a little milk around each pastry triangle to moisten the edges.

Place one sausage along the longest side of each triangle, then roll up towards the point. Set each turnover as you prepare it on the baking tray, with the pastry tip underneath.

Brush each finished turnover with more of the milk and sprinkle with grated cheese.

Place in the centre of a hot oven and bake for 30 minutes. Serve hot with salad.

'Rabbit,' said Pooh to himself, 'I like talking to
Rabbit. He talks about sensible things. He doesn't
use long, difficult words, like Owl. He uses short
easy words, like "What about lunch?" and
"Help yourself Pooh!"'
The House at Pooh Corner

Macaroni Cheese and Tomato

Serves 4

3–4 oz quick cooking macaroni
2 tomatoes
For the cheese sauce:
1 oz butter or margarine
½ pint milk
1 oz (or 1 rounded tablespoon) plain flour
½ level teaspoon salt
pinch of pepper
¼ level teaspoon prepared mustard
4 oz (or 4 heaped tablespoons) grated cheese

Find a large saucepan for cooking the macaroni and a colander to
drain it, a small saucepan, a wooden spoon and a whisk and a
grater for the cheese. Find a 1½-pint pie dish and butter the inside,
and also a pair of oven gloves.

Half fill a large saucepan with water, add the salt and bring up
to the boil. Add the macaroni and when the water reboils, simmer

for 7 minutes. When cooked, drain, rinse under hot water and set aside ready to add to the sauce. Slice the tomatoes.

Place the butter or margarine in a saucepan and set over a low heat to melt. Measure the cold milk into a basin and sift the flour on to it. Using a whisk or rotary hand beater, mix the two together very thoroughly.

Pour the blended milk and flour into the melted fat and cook, stirring all the time until the mixture has thickened and is boiling. Simmer for 2–3 minutes, then season well with salt and pepper, add the mustard and half the cheese. Add the cooked macaroni and mix well. Heat through for a few moments, then draw the pan off the heat.

Pour into the pie dish. Decorate the top with alternate rows of sliced tomato and the remaining grated cheese.

Pass the macaroni cheese under a hot grill until bubbling hot and brown. Serve with hot buttered toast or a salad.

Cottleston Pie

Serves 4
6 oz shortcrust pastry (this can be freshly made or deep frozen)
milk for glazing
For the filling:
4 lean bacon rashers
4 eggs
salt and pepper

Find a pastry board, a rolling pin and a pastry brush. Find a 7–8″ shallow pie plate and butter the inside. Turn on the oven heat to hot (400 °F or Gas No 6) and find a pair of oven gloves.

Prepare the pastry exactly as described in the recipe for Honey tart (see page 84) or use a packet of frozen pastry. Allow the prepared pastry to rest for 5–10 minutes before rolling out.

Divide the pastry in half and set one piece aside. Roll the remaining half out to a circle, slightly larger than the pie plate. Line the plate with the pastry and damp the pastry rim with water.

Cottleston, Cottleston, Cottleston Pie,
A fly can't bird, but a bird can fly.
Ask me a riddle and I reply:
'Cottleston, Cottleston, Cottleston Pie.'
Winnie-the-Pooh

Using a pair of scissors, trim the rinds from the bacon rashers. Arrange the rashers on their sides over the base of the pie, leaving four spaces for the eggs. Break an egg into each space between the rashers. Season each egg with salt and pepper.

Roll out the remaining pastry to a circle large enough to cover the pie. Cut a few slits in the centre, and cover the pie with the pastry. Press the edges firmly together to seal and using a knife trim away the excess pastry.

Brush the pie with a little milk and place in the centre of the preheated oven. Bake for 15 minutes, then lower the heat to moderate (350 °F or Gas No 4) and bake for a further 15 minutes.

Remove from the heat, allow to cool. When cold cut in four portions and serve with salad.

'Well,' said Pooh, 'I've go to go home for something, and so has Piglet, because we haven't had
it yet, and—.'

House at Pooh Corner

Spaghetti Supper

Serves 4

8 oz spaghetti
1 oz butter or margarine
1 medium onion
2 tablespoons tomato purée
1 tablespoon water
grated cheese for serving

Find a large saucepan and a colander for the spaghetti, a knife, a
cutting board and two forks. You will also need a dish for serving
and a grater for the cheese.

Half fill a large saucepan with cold water, add the salt and bring
to the boil. Add the spaghetti, holding it in a bunch as you add it
to the pan. As it softens, wind it round the base of the pan. This
way you will have nice long spaghetti. When the water reboils,
simmer for 12 minutes, then drain in a colander.

Rinse out the pan and replace it over the heat. Add the butter
and allow it to melt. Finely chop the onion and add to the pan.

Cook gently for about 5 minutes until the onion is soft but not brown.

Stir in the tomato purée and the water and then draw the pan off the heat. Add the spaghetti and using two forks, toss and turn the spaghetti so that it is nicely glazed with the hot tomato sauce.

Turn into a heated serving dish and top with grated cheese.

Dessert and Party Recipes

'Pooh,' he said, 'Christopher Robin is giving a party.'

'Oh!' said Pooh. . . . 'Will there be those little cake things with pink sugar icing?'

Winnie-the-Pooh

Apple Crisp

Serves 4

1 lb cooking apples
2 oz (or 2 rounded tablespoons) castor sugar
1 tablespoon water
For the topping:
2 oz butter or margarine
1 rounded tablespoon golden syrup
3 teacupfuls cornflakes

Find a knife for preparing the apples, a saucepan, a wooden spoon and a fork. Choose a 1½-pint pie dish and butter the inside. Turn the oven heat to moderate (350 °F or Gas No 4) and find a pair of oven gloves.

Peel, core and slice the apples. Arrange neatly over the base of the pie dish. Sprinkle with the sugar and add the water.

Place the butter or margarine and syrup in a saucepan. Set over low heat and stir occasionally with a wooden spoon until the butter has melted. Draw the pan off the heat.

He doesn't like honey and haycorns and thistles
Because of the taste and because of the bristles.
And all the good things which an animal likes
Have the wrong sort of swallow and too many spikes.
The House at Pooh Corner

Add the cornflakes all at once. Stir with a fork until the cornflakes are all coated with the syrup mixture. Spoon the mixture over the apples and spread evenly.

Place in the centre of the preheated oven and bake for 20–30 minutes, until the fruit is tender and the topping golden brown. Cool until the topping has become quite crisp and then serve with cream or ice cream.

'That's my tablecloth,' said Pooh, as he began to
unwind Tigger.
'I wondered what it was,' said Tigger.
'It goes on the table and you put things on it.'

The House at Pooh Corner

Bread and Butter Pudding

Serves 4

4 slices of white bread from a large sliced loaf
butter for spreading
1 tablespoon sultanas
2 oz (or 2 rounded tablespoons) castor sugar
2 eggs
½ pint milk
few drops vanilla essence

Choose a 1½-pint pie dish and butter the inside. Find a bowl for
mixing, a whisk, a strainer and a knife. Turn on the oven heat
to hot (375 °F or Gas No 5) and find a pair of oven gloves.

Spread the four slices of bread with butter and press together
in pairs to make two sandwiches. Trim away the crusts and then
cut each sandwich into about 6 cubes.

Place the bread in the pie dish and sprinkle with the sultanas
and the sugar.

Crack the eggs into a bowl and add the milk and vanilla essence. Whisk thoroughly and then strain the mixture into the pie dish. Let the pudding stand for 15 minutes for the bread to swell.

Place the dish in the centre of the preheated oven and bake for 35–40 minutes or until the pudding is risen, firm and golden brown. Serve hot with cream.

Fruit Salad with Honey

Serves 4
$\frac{1}{4}$ pint water
2 rounded tablespoons honey
2–3 pieces pared lemon rind
1 tablespoon lemon juice
2 tablespoons orange juice
For the fruit:
2 eating apples
2 bananas
2 oranges
$\frac{1}{4}$ lb green grapes

Find a saucepan and a wooden spoon, a vegetable parer, a lemon squeezer and a knife for preparing the fruit. Choose a pretty bowl for serving the fruit salad.

Measure the water and honey into a saucepan. Thinly pare a few pieces of lemon rind and add the thin strips of rind to the water. Place over a low heat and bring slowly to the boil, stirring

Pooh was sitting in his house one day, counting his pots
of honey, when there came a knock on the door.
'Fourteen,' said Pooh. 'Come in. Fourteen. Or was it
fifteen? Bother. That's muddled me.'

The House at Pooh Corner

occasionally. Simmer for 1–2 minutes, then draw off the heat and
allow to cool.

Remove the lemon peel and pour the syrup into the serving
bowl. Add the strained orange and lemon juice. Peel, core and
slice the apple and peel and slice the banana. Add the fruit to the
syrup as you prepare it – this way the fruit will stay nice and
white.

Mark the orange peel into quarters, then peel away. Separate
into segments and remove the pips. Wash, halve and deseed the
grapes. Add the grapes and orange to the bowl of fruit.

Stir the fruit and then put to chill for several hours before
serving. Serve with cream or ice cream.

Note: According to the time of year you can use different fruits.
Washed sliced strawberries, stoned halved cherries or sliced
peaches may also be added.

Pancakes

Serves 4
4 oz (or 4 rounded tablespoons) plain flour
pinch of salt
1 egg
½ pint milk
butter for frying
castor sugar and lemons or jam for serving

Find a bowl for mixing, a wooden spoon, a sieve and a small frying pan or omelette pan. Choose a plate for serving and put it to warm. Cut a square of greaseproof paper or foil, sprinkle it with castor sugar ready for the pancakes and put it near the place where you will be working.

Sift the flour and salt into a bowl and make a hollow in the centre. Crack the egg into the well and add about one third of the milk. Using a wooden spoon, stir gently starting in the centre of the bowl and mixing first the egg and milk and then gradually drawing in the flour from around the sides of the bowl. As you

'What shall we do about poor little Tigger?
If he never eats nothing he'll never get bigger.'
The House at Pooh Corner

mix, gradually add a little more milk until about half has been added. Beat the batter very thoroughly and then add the remaining milk. Stir well and then pour into a jug.

Place the frying pan over a moderate heat and add a small piece of butter. When hot, pour in about 2 tablespoons of the batter and tip the pan so that the batter runs all over the base of the pan to make a thin pancake. Fry until the underside is brown, then turn with a knife or toss and cook the second side for a moment.

Tip the pancake out flat on to the sugared paper. Add a little more butter to the hot pan and cook the next pancake. Continue until all the batter is used up – you should get 12 pancakes.

As each pancake is prepared, sprinkle with sugar and lemon juice or jam and roll up. Arrange on a hot plate and keep warm. Serve with wedges of lemon.

'That's funny,' he thought. 'I know I had a jar of honey there. A full jar, full of honey right up to the top, and it had HUNNY written on it, so that I should know it was honey. That's very funny.'

Winnie-the-Pooh

Orange and Honey Sauce for Ice Cream

Serves 4

1 rounded teaspoon cornflour
4 tablespoons cold water
2 oranges
1 tablespoon honey
1 tablespoon seedless raisins

Find a saucepan and a wooden spoon for making the sauce, a grater and a lemon squeezer for the oranges.

Measure the cornflour and the water into a small saucepan. Stir with a wooden spoon to dissolve the cornflour. Grate 1 orange very finely. Squeeze the juice from 2 oranges and strain. Add the rind and juice to the cornflour mixture. Then pour in the honey and the raisins.

Place the pan over a moderate heat and bring up to the boil, stirring all the time. Simmer for 1 minute, then draw the pan off the heat.

Serve hot, or cold with vanilla or chocolate ice cream.

'And I know it seems easy,' said Piglet to himself,
'but it isn't everyone who could do it.'

The House at Pooh Corner

Quick Chocolate Sauce

Makes ½ pint
6 oz (or 6 rounded tablespoons) castor sugar
¼ pint water
2 oz (or 4 rounded tablespoons) cocoa powder

Find a saucepan, a wooden spoon, a hand whisk, and a small
bowl.

Measure the sugar and water into a saucepan. Place over a low
heat and stir until the sugar has dissolved. Bring up to the boil,
simmer for 1 minute and then draw the pan off the heat.

Add the cocoa powder all at once and whisk until the sauce is
smooth. Pour into a small bowl and allow the sauce to cool,
stirring occasionally until it thickens.

Serve the sauce over vanilla ice cream or chocolate ice cream or
use for a frosted chocolate milk drink (see page 119).

Honey Tart

Serves 6

6 oz (or 6 rounded tablespoons) plain flour
pinch of salt
3 oz butter or margarine mixed with vegetable fat
3–4 tablespoons water to mix
For the filling:
3 rounded tablespoons honey (you can also use golden syrup)
2 oz (or 4 rounded tablespoons) fresh white breadcrumbs
little grated lemon rind
1 tablespoon lemon juice

Find a large mixing bowl and a fork for the pastry, a saucepan, a
wooden spoon, a grater and a lemon squeezer for the filling. Find
9″ oven proof tart plate. Grease the tart plate, turn on the oven
heat to hot (400 °F or Gas No 6) and find a pair of oven gloves.

Sift the flour and salt into a mixing bowl. Blend the butter or
margarine and vegetable fat together on a plate using a knife. Add
the fat to the flour. Using the tips of your fingers, rub the fat into

'A lick of honey,' murmured the Bear to himself,
'or – or not, as the case may be.'

Winnie-the-Pooh

the flour until the mixture is like fine crumbs and the fat evenly mixed with the flour.

Sprinkle the water into the bowl and mix with a fork until the pastry clings together making a rough dough, leaving the sides of the basin clean. Turn out on to a floured surface and knead lightly to make a smooth dough. Cover and leave for 5–10 minutes while preparing the filling.

Measure the honey or syrup into a saucepan. Warm over a low heat until the honey is runny. Draw off the heat and stir in the breadcrumbs, a little grated lemon rind and the lemon juice.

Lightly flour the working surface and roll out the pastry to a circle about 1″ larger than the tart plate all round. Cover the plate with the pastry, allowing it to overlap the edges. Press gently all over and then using a knife trim the excess pastry away from around the edge of the plate. Keep the scraps of pastry.

Spoon the honey filling into the centre of the tart and spread evenly over the base. Roll out the pastry scraps thinly and using a knife cut into as many thin strips as you can. Use these strips to make a criss-cross lattice decoration, over the filling in the tart. Mark the pastry rim around the tart plate with the floured prongs of a fork to make a pretty edge.

Place the tart on a high shelf in the preheated oven and bake for 20–25 minutes or until the pastry is brown. Cut in wedges and serve warm.

Orange Trifle

Serves 4–6
1 packet of 4 trifle sponge cakes
1 tin mandarin oranges
water (see recipe)
½ an orange jelly
few chopped walnuts for decoration
For the custard:
2 level tablespoons custard powder
1 oz (or 1 rounded tablespoon) castor sugar
½ pint milk

Find a pretty glass dish for serving the trifle. You will also need a measuring jug, a saucepan, a wooden spoon and a small bowl for mixing the jelly and the custard.

Break the sponge cake into pieces and place in the base of the serving dish. Drain the mandarin oranges, keeping the juice, and put a few oranges aside for decoration. Place the remainder in the dish with the sponge cake. Put the orange juice into a measuring jug and add enough water to make half a pint.

When they had all nearly eaten enough, Christopher Robin
banged on the table with his spoon, and everybody stopped
talking and was very silent, except Roo who was just
finishing a loud attack of hiccups and trying to look as if
it was one of Rabbit's relations.

Winnie-the-Pooh

Place this juice in a saucepan and bring up to the boil. Draw off
the heat and add the orange jelly in pieces. Stir until the jelly has
dissolved; the pan should be hot enough to do this. Allow to cool
slightly, then pour over the sponge cake and leave until the jelly
has set.

Measure the custard powder and sugar into a small basin and
mix to a smooth paste with 2 tablespoons of milk taken from the
half pint.

Place the remaining milk in a saucepan and bring almost to the
boil. Gradually pour into the blended custard powder stirring all
the time. Mix well and return this mixture to the milk saucepan.

Replace the pan over the heat and stir constantly until the
custard is thickened and boiling. Draw off the heat and cool a
little, stirring occasionally to prevent a skin forming.

Pour the custard over the jelly base. Decorate with the reserved
orange sections and a few chopped walnuts. Leave until cold
before serving.

Apple Jelly

Serves 6

2 lb cooking apples
4 oz (or 4 rounded tablespoons) castor sugar
½ pint water
1 orange or lime jelly

Find a knife, a saucepan, a wooden spoon and a sieve for the apple mixture. You will also need a mixing bowl and a pretty bowl for serving the apple jelly.

Peel, core and slice the apples. Measure the sugar and water into a large saucepan and stir over a low heat to dissolve the sugar.

Add the sliced apples, cover the pan with a lid and simmer very gently, stirring occasionally until the apples are quite soft – takes about 10 minutes.

Draw the pan off the heat and add the jelly in pieces. Stir until the jelly has dissolved. The pan should be hot enough to do this.

'Tiggers don't like honey.'
'Oh!' said Pooh, and tried to make it sound Sad
and Regretful. 'I thought they liked everything.'
'Everything except honey,' said Tigger.
                                    The House at Pooh Corner

Pass the contents of the saucepan through a sieve into a mixing
basin. Rub through all the pieces of apple. Stir to mix and then
pour into the serving bowl. Cool, then chill until set firm. Serve
with cream or ice cream.

'What do you like doing best in the world, Pooh?'
'Well,' said Pooh, 'what I like best . . .' and
then he had to stop and think. Because although
Eating Honey was a very good thing to do, there was
a moment just before you began to eat it which was
better than when you were, but he didn't know what it
was called.

The House at Pooh Corner

Chocolate Pudding

Serves 4

1½ oz (or 3 rounded tablespoons) cornflour
1 oz (or 2 rounded tablespoons) cocoa powder
3 oz (or 3 rounded tablespoons) castor sugar
1 pint milk
few drops vanilla essence
chopped walnuts for decoration

Find a small mixing bowl, a saucepan, a wooden spoon and a
bowl for serving.

Measure the cornflour, cocoa powder, and sugar into a small
mixing bowl. Mix to a smooth paste with a little milk taken from
the pint. Take care at this stage that the cornflour is completely
blended.

Heat the remaining milk in a saucepan. When hot but not
boiling, stir into the cornflour paste. Mix well and return to the
milk saucepan. Replace over the heat and stir continuously until
the mixture has thickened and is boiling.

Draw the pan off the heat and stir in the vanilla essence. Pour into a serving dish and sprinkle with chopped walnuts. Serve warm or cold with cream or milk.

'Nobody knows anything about this,' he went on.
'This is a Surprise.'

The House at Pooh Corner

Eskimo Bananas

Makes 8 banana lollies
4 firm ripe bananas
4 oz plain chocolate

Check that there is somewhere that you can put these lollies to
freeze. Ideally they should go in a home freezer, next best would
be the frozen foods compartment in a refrigerator. Then cut out
8 squares of kitchen foil and find 16 plain wooden cocktail sticks.
At a later stage you will need a saucepan and a bowl that fits
snugly over the top for melting the chocolate and an ordinary
table knife.

Select firm ripe bananas, there should be no soft dark marks.
Peel the bananas, and cut each one in half through the middle to
make 8 banana halves. Into the cut end of each one, push two
cocktail sticks close together. Push them fairly well in, leaving a
small end to make the lollie handle.

Place a banana in the centre of each square of foil. Wrap them
up neatly and screw the ends closed. Place them in the freezer and
leave for at least 24 hours until frozen firm.

Break the chocolate into the mixing basin and set this over the saucepan half filled with hot water. Stir occasionally until the chocolate is melted and smooth. Remove the basin from the heat and find the knife for spreading the chocolate.

Carefully unwrap each banana, one at a time and, using the knife, spread a thin layer of chocolate over the surface. Hold the lollie by the stick and as you spread the chocolate it will set firm on the cold surface.

Carefully rewrap the chocolate coated banana in the same piece of foil, screw end closed and replace in the freezer.

Bring them out and give them to your friends as a surprise – they should be eaten when still frozen and quite firm.

Lemon Snow

Serves 4

2 oz (or 4 rounded tablespoons) cornflour
1 pint water
2 lemons
4 oz (or 4 rounded tablespoons) castor sugar
2 egg whites

Find a saucepan, a wooden spoon, a grater, a knife and a lemon squeezer. You will also need a bowl, a whisk and a tablespoon for folding in the egg whites. Find a pretty glass dish for serving the snow.

Measure the cornflour into a saucepan and add the water. Finely grate the lemon rind. Use the finest grater you can so that you grate only the outside yellow skin of the lemon. Add the grated rind to the pan and reserve the lemons.

Stir the contents of the pan with a wooden spoon to make sure that the cornflour is thoroughly blended with the water.

The more it SNOWS-tiddely-pom
The more it GOES-tiddely-pom
The more it GOES-tiddelypom
On snowing.
      The House at Pooh Corner

Place the pan over a moderate heat and stir all the time until the mixture comes up to the boil and thickens. Lower the heat and allow it to simmer for a minute. Draw the pan off the heat.

Cut the lemons in half and squeeze the juice. Add the juice to the pan and the sugar and stir well. Set the pan aside and leave to cool for about ten minutes.

Place the egg whites in a bowl and whisk until stiff. Using a metal tablespoon, fold the egg whites carefully but thoroughly into the lemon mixture so that it looks white and frothy. Pour the 'snow' into a serving dish and leave for several hours until quite cold and set before serving.

Christopher Robin came down from the Forest to the
bridge, feeling all sunny and careless, and just as
if twice nineteen didn't matter a bit, as it didn't on
such a happy afternoon. . . .

The House at Pooh Corner

Summer Pie

Serves 6
8 digestive biscuits
1 level tablespoon castor sugar
1½ oz butter or margarine
For the filling:
1 small tin sweetened condensed milk
¼ pint double cream
2 lemons
¼ lb black grapes

Find a rolling pin, a mixing basin, a saucepan, a tablespoon and a
dessertspoon. Find also a 7″ shallow pie plate, a lemon squeezer
and a grater.

Crush the biscuits with a rolling pin to make fine crumbs and
place the crumbs in a mixing basin. Add the sugar. Melt the
butter in a saucepan over a low heat, draw off the heat and using
a fork stir in the biscuit crumb mixture. Mix well.

Spoon the mixture into the centre of the pie plate. Using the back of a tablespoon, press the mixture over the base and round the sides of the dish to make a biscuit pie crust. Chill in the refrigerator for an hour or so until firm.

Place the condensed milk and cream into a mixing basin. Finely grate the rind of 1 lemon. Squeeze the juice from 2 lemons and strain it. Add to the mixture along with the lemon rind. Stir with a wooden spoon to mix and the mixture will go quite thick in the basin.

Pour the filling into the chilled biscuit pie crust and spread level. Wash, half and deseed the black grapes, and arrange them in a ring around the edge of the pie to decorate.

Chill the pie for several hours for the filling to set firm. Then cut in wedges and serve.

Hipy Papy Bthuthdth Thuthda Bthuthdy Cake

Makes one 7″ cake

4 oz (or 4 rounded tablespoons) self raising flour
1 level teaspoon baking powder
4 oz (or 4 rounded tablespoons) castor sugar
4 oz quick creaming margarine
2 large eggs
few drops vanilla essence
For the filling:
1½ oz butter or margarine
3 oz (or 3 heaped tablespoons) icing sugar, sieved
For the pink sugar icing:
8 oz (or 8 heaped tablespoons) icing sugar, sieved
warm water to mix
few drops cochineal colouring
Birthday candles – as many as is required

'Look at the Birthday cake. Candles and pink sugar.'
Winnie-the-Pooh

This cake is made by a special quick mix method. You must use the soft, quick creaming type of margarine and you must make sure that the margarine and eggs are not cold from the refrigerator. If they are, let them stand at room temperature for an hour or so. Find a large mixing bowl, a sieve and wooden spoon for the cake. Find two 7″ sponge cake tins, grease them and line the base of each with a circle of greaseproof paper. You will also need a small bowl for the icing and filling and a knife for spreading. Turn on the oven heat to moderate (350 °F or Gas No 4) and find a wire cooling tray and a pair of oven gloves.

Sift the flour and baking powder into a large mixing basin. Add the sugar, margarine, eggs and a few drops vanilla essence.

Using a wooden spoon, stir first to blend the ingredients, then beat well for 1 minute until the ingredients are well blended and the mixture feels soft.

Dividing the mixture equally, spoon into the two prepared cake tins and spread level. Place in the centre of the preheated oven and bake for 25–30 minutes or until risen and brown.

Remove the cake from the oven using oven gloves. Turn out of the tins and allow to cool on a wire cooling tray.

Meanwhile prepare the filling. Beat the butter or margarine in a basin until soft. Then gradually beat in the sifted icing sugar a little at a time. When the cake layers are cold, spread the filling between them and set aside ready for icing.

Place the sieved icing sugar in a small bowl. Add a little hot water, teaspoonfuls at a time, until the icing is thin enough to pour over the cake. Don't make the icing too thin. Tint with a drop of pink colouring.

Pour the icing all at once, on to the top of the cake. Using a knife, spread first over the top and then down the sides of the cake. Because the icing is mixed with warm water it will set fairly quickly.

Place the birthday candles around the top of the cake once the icing has set. Write Happy Birthday with a little extra thick icing if you like – but spell it correctly!

Pooh didn't mind for
himself, but when he
thought of all the
honey the bees wouldn't be making,
a cold and misty day always made him feel sorry for them.

The House at Pooh Corner

Honey Baked Bananas

Serves 4

4 ripe bananas
4 rounded teaspoons soft brown sugar
1 lemon
4 teaspoons honey

Cut four large squares of foil, big enough to wrap a banana. Find a grater, a knife and a teaspoon. If the oven is already hot, these can be baked. Otherwise they can be heated under the grill.

Peel the bananas and place each one in the centre of a square of foil. Sprinkle them with the sugar and a little grated lemon rind.

Cut the lemon in half, and squeeze a little juice over each banana. Finally drizzle a teaspoon of honey over each one.

Pick up the edges of the foil and fold over the top of the banana to make a packet. Fold in the ends to seal.

Place the packets, either in a hot oven or under a hot grill. Either way cook them for about 10 minutes. Open the packets carefully and serve the bananas in the foil containers.

Christmas Specialities

On Tuesday, when it hails and snows,
The feeling on me grows and grows. . . .
Winnie-the-Pooh

On Thursday when it starts to freeze
And hoar-frost twinkles on the trees
How very readily one sees
That these are whose – but whose are these?
Winnie-the-Pooh

Frosted Fruits

shiny red apples, pears and black grapes
1 egg white
castor sugar for coating

Find a clean tea-cloth and a small paintbrush. Cut a square of kitchen foil or greaseproof paper for the sugar. Find a pretty dish for serving.

Wash and polish up the apples and pears. Wash and pat dry the grapes. The hard fruit should polish up nicely with a tea-cloth and the choice of definite colours for the fruit will show up the frosting nicely.

Place the egg white in a small bowl and lightly whisk with a fork. Sprinkle plenty of sugar on a square of foil or greaseproof paper to make a bed of sugar.

Using a paint brush dipped in the egg white, streak the surface of one of the apples or pears. Take care not to paint all over, a streaky effect running from the top downwards is much more effective.

Prepare only one fruit at a time and as you finish painting it, roll it in the castor sugar. The sugar will only stick where egg white has been painted on and so will give the streaky, frosted effect. Allow the fruit to dry.

For the grapes, keep in a bunch if possible. Dab the top of each grape with a little egg white, then dip the whole bunch in the sugar. Shake away loose sugar and the bunch will have a frosty effect.

Arrange these frosted fruits, along with other unfrosted fruit and nuts for a pretty table centre piece.

Peppermint Creams

Makes 3 dozen
1 egg white
12 oz (or 12 heaped tablespoons) icing sugar, sieved
few drops peppermint essence

Find a medium-sized bowl and a fork for mixing, a sieve for the icing sugar, and a knife and a board for cutting.

Place the egg white in a mixing bowl and using a fork, whisk until frothy.

Using a wooden spoon, gradually beat in about two thirds of the sifted icing sugar. Add peppermint essence to taste – take care not to add too much.

Turn the mixture out on to a clean working surface and knead in the remaining icing sugar. Check the flavour, if necessary add a little more essence and knead it in.

Divide the mixture in half and shape each half into a long rope about 1″ thick. Dust the working surface with a little extra icing sugar to prevent the mixture sticking.

So they went into Kanga's house, and when Roo had
said, 'Hallo, Pooh,' and 'Hallo, Piglet' once, and
'Hallo, Tigger' twice, because he had never said it
before and it sounded funny, they told Kanga what they wanted,
and Kanga said very kindly, 'Well, look in my cupboard,
Tigger dear, and see what you'd like.'

House at Pooh Corner

On a board and using a knife, cut each portion of peppermint
mixture into $\frac{1}{4}''$ thick slices. Using your fingers shape each one
into a neat round.

Leave the peppermint creams, separated out so that they do not
touch each other for several hours or overnight to set firm.
Note: To separate an egg, carefully crack the egg on to a plate.
Place a tumbler over the yolk and tip the plate so that the white
runs into the mixing basin.

'And the only reason for making honey is so as I can eat it.'
Winnie-the-Pooh

Mincemeat Pies

Makes 12
1 (7½ oz) packet frozen puff pastry, thawed
2 heaped tablespoons mincemeat
1 dessert apple
milk for glazing

Find a pastry board, a rolling pin, a 2½″ plain round cutter, a
knife and a bowl for the filling. You will also need a tray of 12
tartlet tins and a pastry brush. Turn on oven heat to hot (400 °F
or Gas No 6), find a pair of oven gloves and wet the baking tray.

Sprinkle a little flour on the working surface and roll the pastry
out thinly. Allow the rolled out pastry to rest for 10 minutes,
while preparing the filling.

Spoon the mincemeat into a small basin. Peel, core and finely
chop the apple. Add to the mincemeat and mix well.

Using a 2½″ plain round cutter, stamp out 24 circles of pastry
as close together as you can. If necessary reroll the trimmings of
pastry for the last few circles.

Line 12 tartlet tins with half the number of circles. Place a teaspoon of the mincemeat mixture in the centre of each. Damp the edges of the remaining pastry circles and place one over each pie to cover. Gently press pastry edges together to seal, and using a pair of scissors snip 2–3 slits on the tops of each one.

Brush with a little milk and place on a high shelf in the preheated oven. Bake for 20 minutes or until well risen and brown. Dredge with icing sugar and serve.

'. . . just a mouthful of condensed milk or whatnot,
with perhaps a lick of honey. . . .'

Winnie-the-Pooh

Coconut Ice

Makes 3 dozen pieces
1 (6 oz) packet desiccated coconut
4 rounded tablespoons sweetened condensed milk
12 oz (or 12 heaped tablespoons) icing sugar, sieved
few drops cochineal colouring

Find a medium-sized mixing bowl, a wooden spoon and a sieve
for the icing sugar, a plate, a knife and a board for cutting.

Measure the coconut and the icing sugar into a mixing bowl
and mix together.

Add the condensed milk – if the condensed milk is runny you
may need 5 tablespoons. Using your hand mix the ingredients to
a stiff consistency in the bowl. Turn out on to a clean working
surface and knead until smooth.

Divide the mixture in half and to one half add a few drops of
cochineal colouring. Knead the colouring in until the mixture is
evenly coloured. Shape both the pink and white portions into
bars of the same size and press together.

Dust a plate with icing sugar and leave the coconut ice on this for several hours until firm. Then, using a knife, cut into $\frac{1}{4}''$ slices.

'I generally have something now – about this time in the morning,' and he looked wistfully at the cupboard in the corner of Owl's parlour.

Winnie-the-Pooh

Chocolate Fudge

Makes 3 dozen pieces
4 oz plain chocolate
2 oz butter
4 tablespoons evaporated milk
finely grated rind of 1 orange
12 oz (or 12 heaped tablespoons) icing sugar, sieved

Find a large saucepan and a bowl that will fit snugly over the top. A wooden spoon, a sieve for the icing sugar and a 7″ shallow square tin. Line the tin with a strip of greaseproof paper cut the width of the base. Half fill the saucepan with hot water and set the mixing basin over the top.

Break the chocolate into the bowl and add the butter. Leave over the hot water, stirring occasionally until the chocolate has melted and blended with the butter. Remove the basin from the heat.

Add the evaporated milk and the finely grated orange rind and mix well. Gradually beat in the sifted icing sugar. Mix thoroughly to get a smooth fairly stiff mixture.

Spoon the mixture into the prepared tin and spread level. Rough up the surface and leave to set. Turn out of the tin and cut up into squares.

'Well,' said Eeyore that afternoon, when he saw them all walking up to his house, 'this is a surprise. Am I asked too?'

The House at Pooh Corner

Marzipan Dates

Make 2–2½ dozen
2 oz (or 2 heaped tablespoons) icing sugar, sieved
2 oz (or 2 rounded tablespoons) castor sugar
1 (4 oz) packet ground almonds
2 tablespoons lightly mixed egg
little almond essence
little pink colouring
1 box dessert dates
extra castor sugar for coating

Find a medium-sized mixing bowl, a knife and a small saucer to hold the castor sugar for coating.

Mix the sifted icing sugar, the castor sugar and ground almonds together in a mixing bowl. Add the lightly beaten egg and a few drops almond essence. Mix to a smooth firm dough in the bowl, then turn out on to a clean working surface. Sprinkle with a little castor sugar and knead lightly.

Divide the mixture in half. Add a few drops of pink colouring to one half and knead in lightly. Do not over mix the marzipan at this stage otherwise it may become oily and difficult to handle.

Using a small knife, slit the dates and carefully remove the stones, keeping the shape of each date as neat as possible.

Form small pieces of marzipan into shapes similar to the stones and place one inside each date. Roll the stuffed dates in castor sugar so that they look pretty and are no longer sticky to handle.

Hot and Cold Drinks

'Drink up your milk first, dear, and talk afterwards.' So
Roo, who was drinking his milk, tried to say that he could
do both at once . . . and had to be patted on the back and dried
for quite a long time afterwards.

Winnie-the-Pooh

'It's a comforting sort of thing to have,'
said Christopher Robin . . .
            The House at Pooh Corner

Lemon Nectar

Serves 4

3 lemons

2 oz (or 2 rounded
    tablespoons) castor sugar

2 rounded tablespoons honey

1 pint boiling water

ice cubes

Find a vegetable peeler, a large mixing bowl, a lemon squeezer
and a kettle or saucepan. You will also need a strainer, a jug and
glasses and ice cubes for serving.

Thinly pare the rind from the lemons and put the thin strips of
rind in a large mixing bowl with the sugar and honey. Reserve
the lemons.

Measure a pint of water into a kettle or saucepan and bring it to
the boil. Pour the water into the mixing bowl and stir to dissolve
the sugar and honey. Set aside for several hours until cold.

Strain the liquid into a large jug. Squeeze the juice from the
lemons and add it to the jug. Chill until ready to serve, then pour
into tall glasses with ice cubes.

'It's snowing still,' said Eeyore gloomily.
'So it is.'
'And freezing.'
'Is it?'
'Yes,' said Eeyore. 'However,' he said, brightening
up a little, we haven't had an earthquake lately.'

The House at Pooh Corner

Frosted Chocolate

Serves 3
Chocolate syrup – see recipe page 83
1 pint chilled milk
3 scoops vanilla or chocolate ice cream

Find a tablespoon, 3 tumblers and straws for drinking.

Into each glass, measure 2–3 tablespoons of the chocolate
syrup. Half fill the tumbler with chilled milk and stir well.

Add a scoop of ice cream to each one, and then top up with
milk. Serve with straws for drinking.

Cider Cup for a Party

Serves 6

½ pint cider
½ pint lemonade
½ pint undiluted orange squash
1 orange, 1 apple and a few mint leaves for decoration
ice cubes

Find a large jug and a spoon for stirring, and a small knife and a chopping board for preparing the fruit. You will also need glasses and ice cubes for serving.

Measure the cider, lemonade and undiluted orange squash into a large jug.

Wash the orange and then cut into slices including the peel. Wash, core and slice the apple, and wash a few sprigs of mint leaves.

Add the fruit to the jug, stir to mix, then pour into glasses with ice cubes to serve.

'There is an Invitation for you.'
'What's that like?'
'An Invitation!'
'Yes, I heard you. Who dropped it?'
'This isn't anything to eat, it's asking you to
the party. Tomorrow.'

Winnie-the-Pooh

Note: To serve 12, follow the recipe above using a 1 pint bottle
of cider and 1 pint each of lemonade and undiluted orange
squash.

Hot Chocolate for a very Blusterous Day

Serves 3

1 oz (or 1 rounded tablespoon) cocoa powder
1 pint milk
2 rounded tablespoons honey

Find a small basin, a wooden spoon, a saucepan and a whisk. You will also need 3 mugs for serving.

Measure the cocoa powder into a small basin. Mix to a smooth paste with a little milk taken from the pint.

Place the remaining milk in a saucepan and add the honey. Place over the heat and warm gently until the milk is hot and the honey dissolved. Pour a little of the hot milk into the blended cocoa powder whisking well. Pour this back into the milk saucepan.

'Correct me if I am wrong,' he said, 'but am I
right in supposing that it is a very Blusterous
day outside?'

The House at Pooh Corner

Bring the hot chocolate up to the boil, whisking all the time.
Draw the pan off the heat at once – milk quickly boils over. Allow
the hot chocolate to stand for several minutes, or until cool
enough to drink. Pour into mugs and serve.

Orangeade

Serves 6

3 oranges
2 lemons
6 oz (or 6 rounded tablespoons) castor sugar
2 pints water
ice cubes

Find a vegetable parer, a saucepan, a wooden spoon and a strainer. You will also need a knife, a lemon squeezer, a bowl, and eventually glasses and ice cubes for serving.

Thinly pare the rind from the oranges and lemons and place the thin strips of rind in a saucepan with the sugar and water. Reserve the lemons and oranges.

Place the pan over moderate heat, stir to dissolve the sugar and then bring up to the boil. Lower the heat and simmer gently for 15 minutes.

Draw the pan off the heat, strain into a bowl and allow to cool.

Squeeze the juice from the oranges and lemons and add to the orangeade. Stir to mix, then serve in glasses with ice cubes.

I
And all your friends
Sends –
I mean all your friend
Send –
(*Very awkward this, it keeps
going wrong.*)
Well, anyhow, we send
our love
END.

  The House at Pooh Corner

Metric Conversion Table

The following list shows the Imperial measures used in the recipes in this book and their equivalent metric measures balanced to the nearest 5 grammes. If you prefer to work with metric measures you may like to use these as a guide.

Dry Measures

¼ oz	10 grammes	8 oz	225 grammes
½ oz	15 grammes	12 oz	340 grammes
1 oz	30 grammes	1 lb	455 grammes
1½ oz	45 grammes	2 lb	910 grammes
2 oz	55 grammes		
3 oz	85 grammes	*Liquid measures*	
4 oz	115 grammes	¼ pint	142 millilitres
5 oz	140 grammes	⅓ pint	189 millilitres
6 oz	170 grammes	½ pint	284 millilitres
7 oz	200 grammes	1 pint	568 millilitres
		2 pints	1,136 millilitres

Index